Level C

Math Word Problems

Mixed Concepts: Whole Numbers to Percents

SERIES TITLES

Math Word Problems—Whole Numbers and Fractions

Math Word Problems—Decimals and Percents

Math Word Problems—Mixed Concepts: Whole Numbers to Percents

Anita Harnadek

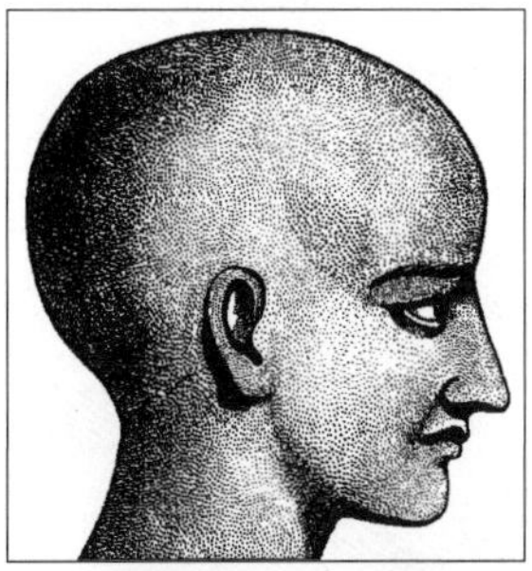

CRITICAL THINKING BOOKS & SOFTWARE

www.CriticalThinking.com

P.O. Box 448 • Pacific Grove • CA 93950-0448

Phone 800-458-4849 • FAX 831-393-3277

ISBN 0-89455-822-6

Printed in the United States of America

Contents

About This Book

The word problems in a general math textbook are almost always grouped so that the student merely has to use the same operation or solution technique for all problems in a group in order to get the answers. What the student needs, and what this book gives, are problems which are arranged so that they cannot be solved by rote processes, which are arranged so that thought and understanding are required. At the same time, we do not want to give word problems which leave students lost in a confusing maze of words and ideas without any clue of how to take a first step toward solving the problem.

We want students to learn when and how to apply their arithmetic knowledge to solving word problems and later to real-life situations, but once the basic concepts are taught, it can be frustrating to search for word problems that fill these needs. Teachers are always looking for word problems that meet the following criteria:

1. The word problems must be at the arithmetic level of the student.
2. They must be at (or below) the reading level of the student.
3. They must be clearly stated.
4. They should be arithmetically mixed so that the student does not automatically add (or divide in a certain order or subtract or whatever) the numbers given in order to get the answer.
5. They should, at least for the most part, be real-life problems requiring practical applications of arithmetic.

The word problems in this book satisfy the above criteria. Designed to spare the teacher the time and trouble of trying to find or create more word problems, and designed to provide the students with practice using various operations with a particular concept or with practice using various operations with various concepts, the problems allow you to give your students the kinds of practice problems they need.

All problems are nongraded in content and are written at an elementary reading level, making them suitable for students at any grade level who have been taught the four basic arithmetic operations.

These problems allow students to use a variety of arithmetic skills in a variety of contexts to solve problems. The result is that the students really learn when and how to apply their arithmetic knowledge to life situations.

And this is what learning arithmetic is all about, isn't it?

Instructions and Answers

Instructions are provided at the beginning of each section. The example problems provided in the instructions can be used as models for solving the problems and to reassure students about what is expected of them in solving the word problems.

Answers for all problems are provided at the back of the book.

About Mixed Concepts 1–3

The problems in Mixed Concepts 1–3 will give the students practice in using not only various operations (addition, subtraction, etc.) but also in using various concepts (whole numbers, fractions, etc.). The problems are mixed so that no one page contains problems which all require the same operation (or series of operations) for solution. One problem might require subtraction of whole numbers, the next require the addition of fractions, the next require computation of a percent, and so on.

Answers given are exact. If you would

rather have your students give approximate answers for some problems, there is no reason not to have them do so.

The difficulty level of the problems moves from easy Mixed Concepts 1 through medium (Mixed Concepts 2) to harder (Mixed Concepts 3). Mixed Concepts 1 can be used starting in elementary school. It can also be used with high school remedial arithmetic students. The problems in Mixed Concepts 2 require a little more thought and would be appropriate for the average high school student or for gifted junior high and elementary school students. The problems in Mixed Concepts 3, too, require only basic arithmetic, but they require more thinking ability than either the Mixed Concepts 1 or the Mixed Concepts 2 problems and, for the most part, they would be too hard for the elementary school level.

The conditions for the problems in these sections are the same as the conditions stated for the problems in the other chapters in this series. That is, the problems are meant to be straightforward arithmetic problems with no missing information.

1. Mixed Concepts 1

INSTRUCTIONS

A. No problem is meant to trick you.

Example

Problem: You buy meat for \$3.87. You give the cashier \$5. How much change do you get?

Answer: \$1.13 (Assume you pay the full price for the meat. Assume you don't buy anything else. Assume there is no sales tax. Assume the cashier gives you the correct change.)

B. You are given all the information you need to solve each problem.

Example

Problem: Oranges sell for 90¢ a dozen. You buy 8 oranges. You give the cashier 75¢. How much change do you get?

Answer: 15¢ (Assume you can buy part of a dozen at the price of 90¢ a dozen. Assume you don't buy anything else. Assume the cashier charges you the right amount. Assume the cashier gives you the right amount of change.)

C. If the answer is a fraction, write it in reduced form.

Example

Problem: Forty people shared 10 pies. How much did each person get?

Answer: $\frac{1}{4}$ pie (We get an answer of $\frac{10}{40}$ pie, which we reduce to $\frac{1}{4}$ pie.)

D. Do not round off any answer unless the problem makes it right to do so.

Example

Problem: Peas sell at 3 cans for $1.01. You buy one can of peas. How much will you be charged?

Answer: $.34 or 34¢ (You can't pay a store a fractional part of one cent.)

E. Assume that a business will always round a part of a cent up, not down, when you are to pay.

Example

Problem: Peas sell at 3 cans for $1. You buy one can of peas. How much will you be charged?

Answer: $.34 or 34¢ (not $.33 or 33¢—Also, you can't pay a store a fractional part of one cent.)

F. If an answer is not about money and if the problem does not tell you how many decimal places to use, then carry the division to two decimal places unless you have a zero remainder before then.

Example

Problem: Write $\frac{49}{16}$ as a decimal.

Answer: $3.06\frac{1}{4}$ (not $3\frac{1}{16}$, not $3.0\frac{5}{8}$, not $3.062\frac{1}{2}$, and not 3.0625)

G. In general, if a percent is not a whole number, write the remainder as a fraction, not as a decimal.

Example

Problem: Rawlins earned $20,000 last year. This year she will earn $24,000. What percent of this year's earnings were last year's earnings?

Answer: $83\frac{1}{3}$% (not 83.3% or 83.33% or 83.333%, etc.)

1. Jan watched 5 TV programs every day for a week. These were the only TV programs she watched. How many TV programs did she watch that week?

2. A large cake was cut into 24 pieces. Each piece was the same size. The cake was shared equally by 8 people. How many pieces did each person get?

3. George, Scott, Sue, Jane, and Charo each wrote a theme for English class. George's theme had 135 words. Scott's had 122 words. Sue's had 113 words. Jane's had 110 words. Charo's had 145 words. What was the total number of words on the five themes?

4. A pet shop has 6 different kinds of kittens. It has 4 kittens of each kind. How many kittens does it have?

5. There are 20 short blocks in a mile. Joy lives 30 short blocks from school. How many miles does Joy live from school?

6. A heavy truck had 6 axles. Five axles each had 4 wheels. The other axle had 2 wheels. What was the total number of wheels the truck had?

7. A school district has two junior high schools. One of these has 536 students. The other has 638 students. What is the total number of students in the junior high schools?

8. A bus started out with only the driver on it. At the first stop, 7 people got on the bus. At the second stop, 2 people got on. At the third stop, 3 people got on and 2 got off. How many people were left on the bus?

9. Mr. Barker works 9 miles from his home. He drives back and forth each day. He works 5 days a week. How far does he drive going back and forth to work each week?

10. Black pencils cost 10¢ each. Red pencils cost 5¢ each. How much does it cost for 2 black pencils and 1 red pencil?

11. A newspaper has 10 comic strips on a page. Each comic strip has 4 pictures. How many comic strip pictures are on the page?

12. A jet flight from Detroit to Los Angeles is 1969 miles. The flight from Los Angeles to San Diego is 109 miles. A passenger gets on at Detroit and gets off at San Diego, but the plane stops first in Los Angeles. How far does the passenger travel?

13. A TV movie was interrupted 5 times each hour for commercials. Four commercials were shown during each interruption. The movie started at 8:00 P.M. and ended at 11:00 P.M. How many commercials were shown during the interruptions?

14. Ace Tallguy is a basketball player. In 5 games, he scored 24, 35, 30, 27, and 34 points. What was the average number of points he scored per game?

15. In another five games, Ace Tallguy scored a total of 170 points. What was the average number of points he scored per game?

16. Jose bought 6 candy bars. Each candy bar weighed 170 grams. What was the total weight of the 6 candy bars?

17. Mr. Black teaches 4 different groups of students. One group has 25 students. Another group has 36 students. Another group has 14 students. The last group has 27 students. How many students are there altogether in the 4 groups?

18. Pop costs 20¢ a bottle. How much do 6 bottles of pop cost?

19. Bob, Joyce, and Mark each have 5 pairs of slacks. What is the total number of pairs of slacks they have?

20. In a baseball diamond, there are 90 feet between bases. How far is it all the way around?

21. A toothpaste test was conducted on 5 groups of 75 people each. How many people were in the test?

22. There were 44 problems on a test Tom took. He missed $\frac{1}{4}$ of them. How many problems did he miss?

23. There were 48 problems on a test Debby took. She missed 25% of them. How many problems did Debby get right?

24. An airliner has 50 rows of seats. Each row has 3 seats on one side, 4 seats in the middle, and 2 seats on the other side. How many seats are in the 50 rows?

25. There are 12 inches in a foot. There are 5280 feet in a mile. How many inches are there in a mile?

26. There are 100 yards between end zones on a football field. How many feet is this?

27. Jake goes to the store. His purchases total $1.29. He gives the cashier $2.00. How much change should he get?

28. Scott's salary is $130 a week. The payroll office withholds $25 for federal income tax, $6.50 for state income tax, and $8.00 for social security tax. What is Scott's net pay each week?

29. The gas tank of your car holds 21 gallons. It is $\frac{1}{3}$ full. How many gallons will it take to fill the tank?

30. Mary earns $4.15 an hour. How much does she earn if she works 35 hours?

31. Emma had scores of 85%, 90%, 70%, and 95% on four tests. What was her average score for these tests?

32. Cass went to the supermarket. He bought bread for 52¢, hamburger for $1.65, and cheese for 93¢. What was the total?

33. Truck tires cost $68 each. The truck has 14 wheels. How much will it cost to buy tires for all the wheels of the truck?

34. Mrs. Corey gets a bill for $50. The bill says she will get a 15% discount if she pays within 10 days. How much will she save if she pays the bill within 10 days?

35. An ad was run on three TV stations. In one night, it was shown 6 times on one station, 3 times on another, and 9 times on the third. What was the total number of times it was shown on the three stations that night?

36. Gasoline costs 79.8¢ a gallon. How much do 15 gallons of gasoline cost?

37. Bread is on sale at 3 loaves for $1.00.

a. How much will 6 loaves of bread cost?

b. You buy 3 loaves. What is the average cost of each loaf?

c. You buy 1 loaf. How much will you be charged?

38. You buy a hamburger for 75¢, a milk shake for 45¢, and french fries for 35¢. What is your total bill?

39. A road map shows a scale of 1 cm = 26 km. You want to drive to a city which is $2\frac{1}{2}$ cm away on the map. How many kilometers away is the city?

40. Bob types an average of 65 words a minute. How many words does he type in 8 minutes?

41. A recipe for a batch of fudge calls for $\frac{3}{4}$ cup of cocoa. How much cocoa should be used for a double batch of fudge?

42. Yancy's car used 24 liters of gasoline for a trip of 300 kilometers. On the average, how many kilometers did the car go for each liter of gasoline used?

43. Mrs. Blue paid $225 for a sofa. When it was delivered, she found a flaw. The store gave her a refund of $30. How much did the sofa cost her?

44. Imported cheese costs $1.70 for a half pound. How much will 2 pounds of the cheese cost?

45. A plane would fly at 700 kilometers an hour if there were no head wind (wind blowing against the plane's direction of travel). How fast will it fly if the head wind is 100 kilometers an hour?

46. Otis telephoned Judy. Judy's phone rang twice. It was 5 seconds from the start of the first ring to the start of the second ring. The phone rang for 1 second each time. How long was the phone silent between the two rings?

47. There are 35 cows and 24 birds standing in a field. All are typical animals. How many legs do they have (total)?

48. Two movies were shown one right after the other. The first one lasted 1 hour and 40 minutes. The second one lasted 2 hours and 35 minutes. How long did it take to show the two movies?

49. A package of cookies contains 26 cookies. Betty wants to have an average of 4 cookies for each of 20 guests. How many packages of cookies should she buy?

50. Two cats each had 5 kittens. Each of the kittens later had 4 kittens. What was the total number of the kittens' kittens?

51. Lila typed 720 words in 12 minutes. What was her average number of words a minute?

52. A jetliner traveling from New York City to Los Angeles flew at an altitude of 35,000 feet. How many miles high (to the nearest tenth) did it fly?

53. The area of a room is 24 square meters. How many square centimeters is this?

54. The usual price on a CD you want is $11.70. It will be on sale next week for $\frac{1}{3}$ off. How much will you save if you wait until next week to buy the CD?

55. Mr. Dakker wants to plant alyssum seeds along a 40-foot border of his lawn. He figures that each package of seeds will cover 5 feet. How many packages of seeds should he buy?

56. A farmer sells two hogs at 20¢ a pound. One hog weighs 465 pounds. The other weighs 375 pounds. How much does the farmer get, in all, for the two hogs?

57. The Nile River in Africa is the longest river in the world. It has a length of 4132 miles. The Ob-Irtysh River is the longest river in Asia. It has a length of 3461 miles. How much longer is the Nile River than the Ob-Irtysh River?

58. To make coffee, Mr. Jackson uses $\frac{3}{4}$ of a tablespoon of coffee for each cup. He uses another tablespoon of coffee "for the pot." How many tablespoons of coffee will he use if he makes 10 cups of coffee in the pot at one time?

59. You buy a suit for $60 plus 4% sales tax. What is the total amount that you pay?

60. A car travels 200 kilometers in $2\frac{1}{2}$ hours. What is its average speed?

61. There are about 2,000 factories in the Baltimore area. These factories make about $3 billion in goods yearly. What is the average value of the goods made yearly by each of these factories?

62. A car travels at an average speed of 60 kph for $3\frac{3}{4}$ hours. How far does it travel in this time?

63. Each day for a year Joe ate 3 meals and 4 snacks. What was the total number of meals and snacks Joe ate that year?

64. You make $3.76 an hour when you work. You work $23\frac{1}{2}$ hours one week. How much do you make that week?

65. Rose went to the Post Office. She bought eleven 15¢ stamps, four 12¢ stamps, and six 20¢ stamps. What was the total she paid for the stamps?

66. You have a sheet of paper. You tear it in half. You stack the pieces and then tear the stack in half. Again you stack the pieces and tear the stack in half. How many pieces of paper do you have now?

67. Ms. Worth is an attorney. She charges $70 an hour for consultation. What is her charge to a client who consulted with her for 4 hours?

68. The college bookstore sold 75 books today for a total of $688.50. What was the average selling price of each book?

69. Mount Everest in Asia is the highest mountain in the world. It is 29,028 feet high. The highest mountain in North America is Mount McKinley (Denali) in Alaska. Its height is 20,320 feet. How much higher is Mount Everest than Mount McKinley?

70. Each roll of candy contains 20 pieces of candy. How many pieces of candy are in 19 rolls?

71. Oranges sell at $1.75 a dozen. If you buy a dozen at a time, what is the average price of an orange?

72. The year before last Kim was 122 cm tall. Last year she was 126 cm tall. This year she is 132 cm tall. How much taller is Kim now than she was two years ago?

73. Gasoline sells for 20.2¢ a liter. How much will 55 liters cost?

74. A store is having a 1¢ sale on pencils. The regular price of a pencil is 15¢. For every pencil Jerry buys at the regular price, he can buy another one for only 1¢.

a. How much will Jerry have to pay if he buys 15 pencils?

b. How much will Jerry have to pay if he buys 16 pencils?

75. A standard badminton court is 20 feet wide and 44 feet long. What is its area?

76. On May 4, 1961, two U.S. Navy men rose to 113,739.9 feet in a balloon. To the nearest tenth, how many miles high was this?

77. At birth, a baby's head is about $\frac{1}{4}$ the length of the rest of its body. A newborn baby's total length is 50 cm.

a. How long is its head?

b. How long is the rest of its body?

78. An average baby weighs about 3 kilograms at birth. It will double its birth weight within six months and will triple it in about a year. How much will an average baby weigh at the end of

a. Six months?

b. About a year?

79. A shop class has 10 girls and 15 boys. What percent of the class is girls?

80. The city of Triticum produces more flour yearly than any other city in the United States. There are 24 grain elevators in Triticum. These elevators can store more than 70 million bushels of grain. On the average, how much grain can each Triticum elevator store?

81. The city of Oswald has about 450 plants which, combined, employ more than 60,000 people. What is the average number of people employed in an Oswald plant?

82. There are 2.54 centimeters in an inch. How many centimeters are there in 15 inches?

83. Four people chipped in equal amounts to buy a large pizza. The pizza cost $4.60.

a. How much did each person chip in?

b. The pizza was cut into 8 pieces. Each person ate 2 pieces. What was the average cost of a piece of pizza?

84. Not counting Alaska, the area of the continental United States is about 12 times the area of Burma. Burma's area is 678,033 square kilometers. About how big is the area of the continental United States, not including Alaska?

85. A printer uses a single sheet of paper to make 4 pages in a book. (Each sheet is folded in half and is printed on both sides of both halves.) How many sheets of paper does he need to make a 580-page book?

86. In the U.S., there are about 320,000 school buses which carry about 20,000,000 students back and forth to school each year. On the average, how many students does each bus carry?

87. Mr. Joyan stayed at a hotel in a state that has a tax of 8% on room rentals. The rental charge totaled $105, not including the tax. How much was the tax?

88. A centrifuge turns 6000 times a minute. How many times a second does it turn?

89. Gasoline sells for 19.6¢ a liter. How many liters (to the nearest tenth) can you buy for $12?

90. Kleland, a small country, has about 4,000,000 people. Only about 5% of the people can read and write. About how many people in Kleland cannot read and write?

91. The population of East Metropolis is about 1,087,450. The population of West Metropolis is about 2,136,500. What is the total population of Metropolis?

92. A typist bought some typing supplies. She paid $4.75 for a ream of paper. She paid $2.35 for a typewriter ribbon. She paid 20¢ for a typewriter eraser. Altogether, how much did she spend on these supplies?

93. A serving of peas weighs 75 grams. How many servings are in a 900-gram can of peas?

94. A particular city has about 745 industrial plants. These plants manufacture $540 million in goods annually. To the nearest cent, what is the average value of the goods manufactured by a plant in this city?

95. There are 6 telephone cables across the Atlantic Ocean. Each can carry 138 conversations at once. How many telephone conversations can the 6 cables handle all at once?

96. The Panama Canal was completed in 1914 at a cost of about $380 million. It is about 81.6 kilometers long. What was the average cost per kilometer?

97. There are 13 islands in the Canary Islands, but only 7 are inhabited. What percent are inhabited?

98. The 13 Canary Islands have a total area of 7273 square kilometers. On the average, what is the area of one of the Canary Islands?

99. The 7 populated Canary Islands have a total of about 1,200,000 people. On the average, about how many people live on each of these 7 islands?

100. The wax of the berries of the candleberry shrub is used for making candles. A bushel of berries yields about 2 kilograms of wax. How many bushels of berries would be needed to yield about 75 kilograms of wax?

101. A rectangle is 20 cm by 30 cm. There is a border all around it which is 4 cm wide. What are the dimensions of the rectangle and the border together?

102. In 1861, the population of Chattanooga, Tennessee, was 5545. In 1975, it was 119,923. By how much did Chattanooga's population increase from 1861 to 1975?

103. A circular swimming pool has a radius of 4 meters. What is its circumference? (Use $\pi = 3.1416$.)

104. Five monkeys climbed coconut trees and started throwing coconuts at each other. The first monkey threw 17 coconuts. The second threw 15. The third threw 20. The fourth threw 13. The fifth threw 25. What was the total number of coconuts thrown?

105. What's the difference (if any) between an area described as "4 kilometers square" and an area described as "4 square kilometers"?

106. Forests cover about 43% of California's 411,013 square kilometers. About how much area do these forests cover?

107. In 1974, Chemical & Engineering News reported figures for Exxon Corporation as follows: total sales, $25,724,000,000; chemical sales, $1,563,000,000. According to these figures,

a. how much more were Exxon's total sales than its chemical sales?

b. what percent of Exxon's total sales were its chemical sales?

108. Canada has about 23,000,000 people. About 76% of the people live in cities.

a. What percent of Canada's people do not live in cities?

b. How many people is this?

109. There are about 25 million books, pamphlets, and periodicals in 700 public libraries. Suppose that each of these libraries has the same number of books, etc. Then about how many books, etc. are in each library?

110. Small Country's population is estimated at 9,125,000. Its population density is $82\frac{1}{4}$ people per square kilometer. To the nearest whole number, what was the area of Small Country?

111. A math class of 27 students has 12 boys. What percent of the class is girls?

112. Tammy built a birdhouse for a robin. She made the floor 18 cm square. She made the house 19 cm high. What was the volume of the robin's house?

113. A map is drawn to a scale of 1 cm = 118 km. How many km apart are two towns which are $4\frac{1}{2}$ cm apart on this map?

114. In 1939, Berlin's population was about 4,340,000. In 1945, it was about 2,800,000. By how much did Berlin's population decrease in these six years?

115. Ms. Edding bought 6 dozen eggs for a total of $7.00. What was the average price of each egg?

116. Ms. Felding went golfing. Par on the front 9 holes was 68. Par on the back 9 holes was 67. Ms. Felding's score on the front 9 holes was 72. Her score on the back 9 holes was 70. Was her score over par or under par, and by how much was it over or under?

117. It took Ms. Jotwin 5 hours to drive her car 350 km. What was the car's average speed during this time?

118. Mr. Atkins drove his car for 4 hours at an average speed of 80 kph. How far did his car go in this time?

119. Isaac went to a school carnival. He bought 5 tickets at 10¢ each, 4 tickets at 25¢ each, and 10 tickets at 5¢ each. What was the total cost of the tickets he bought?

120. The cost of a pony ride at the school carnival was 50¢. At the end of the carnival, the total amount collected for pony rides was $153.50. No one had a free pony ride. How many pony rides were there?

121. The school carnival also had a "car smash." For 25¢, a person could smash at the car three times with a sledgehammer. The "car smash" collected a total of $109.75. No one hit the car without paying. Everyone who paid hit the car exactly three times.

a. How many people hit the car?

b. How many times was the car hit?

122. Ms. Sims is a mail delivery person. She walks an average of 11 miles a day on her job. She works an average of 220 days a year. What is the average number of miles Ms. Sims walks on her job in a year?

123. Ms. Wilson ran two want ads in the local newspaper. The cost of one ad was $4.65. The cost of the other ad was $3.15. What was the total cost of the two ads?

124. Mr. Jackson bought a used van for $1500. He gave a deposit of $250. How much did he still owe?

125. Suki's school collected 15,000 pounds of paper during a paper drive. The paper company paid $1.45 for each 100 pounds of paper. How much money did the school get for the paper collected?

126. A restaurant has a special lunch. The lunch sells for $3 for an adult's portion and $2 for a child's portion. How much will the restaurant charge for 11 adults' portions and 15 children's portions?

127. Hamburger contains 28% fat. You buy 10 kilograms of hamburger. All the fat cooks away when you fry the hamburger. How many kilograms of meat will you have after you fry the hamburger?

128. A $\frac{1}{4}$-grain tablet of saccharin has the sweetening power of 1 teaspoonful of sugar. How much sweetening power does a 1-grain tablet of saccharin have?

129. Ms. Brooks bought 40 liters of gasoline at 17.1¢ a liter. She also bought 4 liters of oil at $1.33 a liter. How much did she spend in all?

130. A filing clerk filed 15 cards under "A." He filed 11 cards under "C." He filed 25 cards under "M." He filed 3 cards under "Y." He did not file any other cards. What was the total number of cards he filed?

131. A hummingbird egg is about 13 mm long. An ostrich egg is about 15 cm long. What percent of the length of an ostrich egg is the length of a hummingbird egg?

132. The average weight of an elephant's brain is 5000 grams. The average weight of a man's brain is 1400 grams. What percent of the average weight of an elephant's brain is the average weight of a man's brain?

133. When you eat at a restaurant, it is usual to tip the waiter or waitress 15% of the meal charge. Edith ate at a restaurant yesterday. Her meal charge was $3.60. She also left the usual tip. How much was the tip she left?

134. Four years ago Kyle's salary was $6,500. Three years ago it was $7,500. Two years ago it was $11,000. Last year it was $14,000. This year Kyle's salary will be $17,000. What is Kyle's average salary over these years?

135. California has 5 state-supported colleges and 14 state-supported universities. About 300,000 students are enrolled in these. On the average, how many students are enrolled at each of these colleges and universities?

136. A rectangle has a width of $3\frac{1}{2}$ feet and a length of $5\frac{1}{4}$ feet. What is the distance all the way around it?

2. Mixed Concepts 2

INSTRUCTIONS

A. No problem is meant to trick you.

Example

Problem: You buy meat for $3.87. You give the cashier $5. How much change do you get?

Answer: $1.13 (Assume you pay the full price for the meat. Assume you don't buy anything else. Assume there is no sales tax. Assume the cashier gives you the correct change.)

B. You are given all the information you need to solve each problem.

Example

Problem: Oranges sell for 90¢ a dozen. You buy 8 oranges. You give the cashier 75¢. How much change do you get?

Answer: 15¢ (Assume you can buy part of a dozen at the price of 90¢ a dozen. Assume you don't buy anything else. Assume the cashier charges you the right amount. Assume the cashier gives you the right amount of change.)

C. If the answer is a fraction, write it in reduced form.

Example

Problem: Forty people shared 10 pies. How much did each person get?

Answer: $\frac{1}{4}$ pie (We get an answer of $\frac{10}{40}$ pie, which we reduce to $\frac{1}{4}$ pie.)

D. Do not round off any answer unless the problem makes it right to do so.

Example

Problem: Peas sell at 3 cans for $1.01. You buy one can of peas. How much will you be charged?

Answer: $.34 or 34¢ (You can't pay a store a fractional part of one cent.)

E. Assume that a business will always round a part of a cent up, not down, when you are to pay.

Example

Problem: Peas sell at 3 cans for $1. You buy one can of peas. How much will you be charged?

Answer: $.34 or 34¢ (not $.33 or 33¢—Also, you can't pay a store a fractional part of one cent.)

F. If an answer is not about money, and if the problem does not tell you how many decimal places to use, then carry the division to two decimal places unless you have a zero remainder before then.

Example

Problem: Write $\frac{49}{16}$ as a decimal.

Answer: $3.06\frac{1}{4}$ (not $3\frac{1}{16}$, not $3.0\frac{5}{8}$, not $3.062\frac{1}{2}$, and not 3.0625)

G. In general, if a percent is not a whole number, write the remainder as a fraction, not as a decimal.

Example

Problem: Rawlins earned $20,000 last year. This year she will earn $24,000. What percent of this year's earnings were last year's earnings?

Answer: $83\frac{1}{3}$% (not 83.3% or 83.33% or 83.333%, etc.)

1. Your car's gas tank holds 100 liters of gasoline. You fill the tank. You drive 400 kilometers. It takes 80 liters to fill the tank again. How far did your car go for each liter of gasoline used?

2. Marguerita bought 3 blouses for a total of $15.50. She found a flaw in one later and returned it to the store. The store gave her a full refund, $4.74. What was the average price of the blouses she kept?

3. A supermarket's cost of groceries averages 86% of the selling price. One day the market sells a total of $4187.60 in groceries. How much profit did the market make on the groceries that day?

4. The yearly finance charge on a used car is 16% of the original unpaid balance. You buy the car for $5000. You pay $1000 down (no trade-in). You agree to pay off the car over a three-year period. What will the total finance charge be?

5. A room without windows is 12 feet wide and 16 feet long. The ceiling is 8 feet high. What is the wall area of the room, including doorways?

6. You make $5.62 an hour. You work 40 hours one week. The payroll office takes the following amounts from your pay: 18% for federal income tax; 5% for state income tax; 6.1% for social security tax; 1% for union dues. Give the amount of each of the following: gross pay, federal income tax, state income tax, social security tax, union dues, net pay.

7. Roy wants to invite 7 friends to his house. He wants to serve them hamburgers. He figures he can make 5 hamburgers from each pound. He figures he and his friends will each eat 4 hamburgers. Hamburger costs $1.15 a pound.

a. How many pounds should he buy?

b. How much will it cost?

8. To figure typing speed (in words a minute), count the total number of characters typed (including spaces). Then divide by five. And then divide by the number of minutes typed. Randy typed 1500 characters in 6 minutes. What was his typing speed?

9. Bank A pays 3/4% more in yearly interest than Bank B. How much more interest will $5000 earn in a year in Bank A than in Bank B?

10. Bacteria are found almost everywhere. It is thought that the air may have more than 100 bacteria in each cubic foot. If so, how many bacteria might there be in a school room 20 feet wide by 30 feet long if the ceiling is 12 feet high?

11. A picture is 42 cm long and 32 cm wide. It has a 5 cm wide frame around it. All around the picture, 1 cm of the picture sticks into the frame so that the frame can hold it. What is the area of the frame?

12. There are 330 people in one company and 250 people in another company. The two companies got together to form a bowling league. One sixth of the people from the first company joined the league. From the second company, 10% joined the league. How many people were in the bowling league?

13. Ms. Wemming is going to buy a refrigerator. The price is $375 if she pays cash. If she makes monthly payments, she must pay $80 down and then pay $28.27 a month for 12 months. Which way of paying will cost her less? How much less?

14. On a series of plays, the Detroit Lions gained 9 yards on a first down, lost 3 yards on the second down, gained a yard on the third down, and gained 5 yards on the fourth down. On the next series of plays, they gained 4 yards on the first down, gained 2 more on the second down, lost 3 yards on the third down, and gained 5 yards on the fourth down. What was their average gain per down on these two series of plays?

15. Two brands of tomatoes are of equal quality. One brand sells at three 400-gram cans for 79¢, and the second brand sells at two 650-gram cans for 87¢. Which brand is the better buy?

16. A state law says a minor may not spend more than 48 hours a week going to school and working. Martha attends school from 7:45 A.M. to 1:15 P.M. each day Monday through Friday. She also works afternoons at a restaurant. What is the maximum number of hours the state law allows Martha to work in a week (during the school year, not counting vacations)?

17. Mr. Johnson's salary is $270 a week. How much is his monthly salary?

18. Mr. Jones wants to paint the walls in three rooms white. In one room, the wall area is 336 square feet. In another room, the wall area is 400 square feet. The wall area of the third room is 364 square feet. A gallon of paint covers 300 square feet. How many gallons of paint should Mr. Jones buy to do the job? (Assume that partial gallons of paint are not sold.)

19. In Ms. Doan's class, 40% of the class are boys; 60% of Mr. Fry's class are boys. There are 25 students in Ms. Doan's class and 30 students in Mr. Fry's class. No boy is in both classes. How many boys are in these classes?

20. Marinda bought six bottles of pop for a total of $2.50, including bottle deposits totaling $1.20. What was the average price of each bottle of pop, not including the bottle deposit?

21. A pound of gold contains 12 ounces (apothecaries' weight or troy weight). A pound of feathers contains 16 ounces (avoirdupois weight or U.S. customary system). Given the different systems of measurement, which is heavier—16 pounds of gold or 12 pounds of feathers if

a. an ounce in either system weighs the same amount?

b. an ounce in apothecaries' weight is heavier than an ounce in avoirdupois weight?

22. The charges for running a 15-second ad on a TV station are as follows:

$200 from 12:00 A.M. to 6:30 A.M.
$300 from 6:30 A.M. to 9:00 A.M.
$350 from 9:00 A.M. to 11:00 A.M.
$400 from 11:00 A.M. to 3:30 P.M.
$450 from 3:30 P.M. to 6:00 P.M.
$500 from 6:00 P.M. to 8:00 P.M.
$600 from 8:00 P.M. to 11:00 P.M.
$500 from 11:00 P.M. to 11:30 P.M.
$400 from 11:30 P.M. to 12:00 A.M.

a. Big Corporation runs 15-second ads on the station as follows:

3 ads from 9:00 A.M. to 11:00 A.M.
5 ads from 11:00 A.M. to 2:00 P.M.
6 ads from 8:00 P.M. to 11:00 P.M.

How much does Big Corporation owe the station for these ads for one day?

b. Hit Records runs 15-second ads on the station as follows:

15 ads from 12:00 A.M. to 6:30 A.M.
5 ads from 6:30 A.M. to 9:00 A.M.

How much does Hit Records owe the station for these ads for one day?

23. Jay worked one day from 9:12 A.M. to 3:45 P.M. How long did he work that day?

24. Jenny worked one day from 9:45 A.M. to 3:12 P.M. How long did she work that day?

25. In the two problems above, who worked longer (Jay or Jenny?), and how much longer did he or she work?

26. A barber charges $6.25 for a haircut and $3.50 for a shave. Last Tuesday, he shaved 19 customers and cut the hair of 21 customers. What was the total amount he charged for these services?

27. Art decided to walk in the March of Dimes Walkathon. He had a total of 53 sponsors, and 28 of them each pledged 10¢ a mile. The other sponsors each pledged 25¢ a mile. Art walked 20 miles in the Walkathon. How much (total) should he collect from his sponsors?

28. In 1975, the population of Brazil was estimated at about 107,702,000. It was also estimated that about $\frac{3}{4}$ of the people lived along the Atlantic coast in a strip 480 kilometers wide. Also, about 62% of the total population was urban, and about 38% was rural.

a. About how many Brazilians lived within the Atlantic coast strip?

b. About how many Brazilians lived in cities?

c. About how many Brazilians lived in rural areas?

29. A man owns two hotels. One has 436 rooms. The other has 362 rooms. On an average day, $\frac{2}{3}$ of the rooms are occupied.

a. What is the total number of rooms occupied in this man's hotels on an average day?

b. What is the total number of rooms unoccupied in this man's hotels on an average day?

30. In baseball, a player's batting average is figured by dividing the number of hits by the number of times at bat. A sacrifice is not counted as a time at bat. Tiger Walton has batted 33 times so far this season. He struck out 3 times, sacrificed 4 times, hit 3 flies caught by fielders, grounded out 14 times, hit 15 foul balls, hit 3 home runs, hit 2 doubles, and hit singles the other times. To three decimal places, what is his batting average so far this season?

31. In a war battle, an Army battalion, 880 people, was made up of four companies. Each company was made up of five platoons. Each platoon contained four squads. Each company had the same number of people, as did each platoon and each squad. How many people were in each squad?

32. Suppose that each squad in the army contains 12 people. A platoon contains 5 squads. A company contains 6 platoons. A battalion contains 3 companies. A brigade contains 4 battalions. How many people are in a brigade?

33. You buy a dozen oranges at 3 for 47¢. You also buy $1\frac{1}{2}$ pounds of potatoes at 26¢ a pound. What is your total bill for these items?

34. Two salesmen were competing for a prize. The prize was to go to whoever had the most sales in a week. Following is the record of their sales for the week.

Day	Salesman 1	Salesman 2
1	$1,056.27	none
2	537.65	$956.78
3	784.97	877.60
4	422.11	none
5	217.85	988.90
6	335.22	869.70
7	325.90	none

a. What was the total of the sales by salesman 1?

b. What was the total of the sales by salesman 2?

c. Who won the contest?

35. A room measures 4 meters by $5\frac{1}{2}$ meters. What is its area in square centimeters?

36. Gold jewelry is not usually pure gold but is an alloy of gold and other metals. One carat of gold means that $\frac{1}{24}$ of the total weight of the alloy is gold.

a. A ring is 14-carat gold. What fraction of the alloy in the ring is gold?

b. A watch case is 10-carat gold. What percent of the alloy in the watch case is gold?

37. A discount movie theater charges $2.50 for an adult's ticket. It charges $1.75 for a child's ticket. How much will the theater collect if it sells 115 adults' tickets and 198 children's tickets?

38. Peas sell for 2 cans for 55¢. The selling price of a 24-can case of peas is $6.20. Mr. Whitney and Ms. Janning both used 24 cans of peas over a 4-month period. Mr. Whitney bought them 2 at a time. Ms. Janning bought a case. Who paid more, and how much more?

39. The Standard Oil Building in Chicago is 1136 feet tall and has 80 stories. The John Hancock Center in Chicago is 1107 feet tall and has 100 stories.

a. What is the average number of feet per story (to the nearest hundredth) of the Standard Oil Building?

b. What is the average number of feet per story (to the nearest hundredth) of the John Hancock Center?

c. To the nearest tenth, what percent of the Standard Oil Building's height is the John Hancock Center's height?

d. To the nearest tenth, what percent of the average story height of the Standard Oil Building is the average story height of the John Hancock Center?

e. Suppose that the average story height of the Standard Oil Building were the same as that of the John Hancock Center. How tall (to the nearest foot) would the Standard Oil Building be?

f. Suppose that the average story height of the John Hancock Center were the same as the average story height of the Standard Oil Building. How tall (to the nearest foot) would the John Hancock Center be?

40. A travel agency gets a 10% commission on each airline ticket it sells. It gets a 15% commission on each hotel reservation it makes (provided that the reservation is kept, of course). One month it sells a total of $5,724.80 in airline tickets and it makes hotel reservations totaling $2,435.00, all of which are kept. How much does it earn in commissions?

41. A house plan has a scale of $\frac{1}{4}$ inch = 1 foot. When a room 12 feet by 15 feet is drawn on this house plan, what will its house plan dimensions be?

42. The area of Ethiopia is 471,778 square miles or 1,221,000 square kilometers. The area of Tanzania is 364,900 square miles or 945,087 square kilometers.

a. Use the areas in square miles. What percent (to the nearest tenth) of Ethiopia's area is Tanzania's area?

b. Use the areas in square kilometers. What percent (to the nearest tenth) of Ethiopia's area is Tanzania's area?

43. A savings bank pays interest at the rate of 6% a year. Each quarter they compute the interest earned for that quarter and they add it to the balance. If you put $1,000 in the bank on December 31st and do not make any withdrawals or any more deposits, how much will you have as of the end of December 31st of the next year?

44. Mr. Harris rented a power rake for his yard. The charge was $5.00 for the first hour and $3.50 an hour (or any part of an hour) for each hour after the first hour. He checked the power rake out at 10:12 A.M. He checked it back in at 2:28 P.M. How much did he owe for the rental?

45. Becky likes two kinds of potato chips—Crunchies and Krispys. A 340-gram bag of Crunchies sells for 99¢. A 340-gram bag of Krispys sells for $1.10. The Krispys are never burned or broken up. About $\frac{1}{10}$ of the Crunchies are always burned or broken up, and Becky always ends up throwing this $\frac{1}{10}$ out. Which brand should she buy in order to get the most for her money?

46. Each year, about $1,750,000,000 of ore is mined in California. This is about 5% of the total yearly value of goods produced in California. About how much is California's total yearly value of goods produced?

47. Most high school basketball courts are 84 feet by 50 feet. Most college and professional basketball courts are 94 feet by 50 feet. The area of the usual high school basketball court is what percent (to the nearest tenth) of the area of the usual professional basketball court?

48. A car's gas tank holds 90 liters. You fill the tank when the car's odometer shows 23,092.4 (kilometers); the gas tank takes 70 liters. The next time gas is needed, it takes 60 liters to fill the tank, and the odometer shows 23,635.1. What is the average number of kilometers (to the nearest tenth) traveled for each liter of gas used?

49. Joy's age is 15 years 6 months. Frank's age is 14 years 7 months. Randall's age is 17 years 8 months. What is the average age of these three people?

50. A telephone company bills phone calls by distance in four ways: local, near zone, far zone, and long distance. A "near zone" dialed call costs 4.3¢ a minute. A "far zone" dialed call costs 7.9¢ a minute. Any part of a minute counts as a full minute. On both kinds of calls there is an added charge of 1.5¢ a call if operator assistance is required.

a. John asks the operator to dial a "near zone" number for him. When his party answers, they talk for 3 minutes 15 seconds. What is the charge for John's call?

b. Josita dials a call to the "far zone." When her friend answers, they talk for 15 minutes 25 seconds. What is the charge for Josita's call?

51. You work at your job for a weekly salary of $80 plus 3% commission on all the sales you make. You make sales of $9,000 one week. How much altogether do you earn that week at your job?

52. A honeybee flies at a speed of about 12 miles an hour. About how many feet does it fly in one second?

53. Aluminum comes from bauxite ore. In Jamaica, 1200 tons of bauxite ore were mined. Of this 1200 tons, 564 tons were aluminum, 42 tons were silica, 24 tons were titanium oxide, 264 tons were iron oxide, and the rest was water. Tell what percent of the ore was made up of each part named above.

54. An income tax schedule shows the following:

If your taxable income is		
at least	**but less than**	**then your tax is**
0	$2,000	14% of your taxable income
$2,000	$4,000	$280 + 18% of the excess over $2,000
$4,000	$6,000	$640 + 22% of the excess over $4,000

a. How much is the income tax on a taxable income of $500?

b. How much is the income tax on a taxable income of $2,300?

c. How much is the income tax on a taxable income of $5,800?

55. A cash register started out with $20 in bills and change. Sales totaled $1,027.35, of which $548.50 was for charge sales and the rest for cash sales. Money was taken out as follows: $368.50 to pay for expenses; $50 to put in the petty cash fund. Also, another $35 was put in because the register was running short of change, and the store collected $100 on old charge sales. How much cash should have been in the register at this point?

56. Beefsteak contains 18.7% protein and 17% fat. Suppose a beefsteak weighs 250 grams. How many grams will be

a. protein?

b. fat?

57. Suppose 15 people pick 12 bushels of oranges and divide them evenly among themselves. How many bushels does each person get?

58. The Carlsbad Caverns National Park in New Mexico became a national park in 1930. At that time, the area above ground was 700 acres. By the start of 1975, much more area had been added to the park, and the area above ground was 46,753 acres.

a. By what percent did the area of the park increase from 1930 to 1975?

b. What was the average percent of increase each year? (Do not include 1930 or 1975.)

59. A family spends $\frac{1}{4}$ of its total income for housing. Of the housing amount, 1/5 is spent for utilities. The total income is $21,000 a year. How much a year is spent for utilities?

60. At noon, a gas station's pumps showed that the station had sold 513 gallons of regular gas and 625 gallons of lead-free gas. Regular gas sold for 72.1¢ a gallon. Lead-free gas sold for 76.3¢ a gallon. How much were the total gas sales as of noon?

61. In the United States, about 1,000 bus companies operate more than 22,000 intercity buses. Each year, the buses travel about 1,600,000,000 kilometers and carry about 400,000,000 riders. What is the average number of

a. buses each bus company operates?

b. riders each bus company carries yearly?

c. kilometers each bus company's buses travel yearly?

d. kilometers each bus travels yearly?

e. riders each bus carries yearly?

f. kilometers each rider travels yearly?

62. In Canada, mining accounts for 17%, about $5,750,000,000, of the value of all goods produced. About how much is the total value of Canadian goods produced?

63. The formula $d = 4.8768t^2$ gives the number of meters an object will fall freely in t seconds, ignoring air resistance. Suppose a ball is dropped from the top of the Empire State Building. Ignoring air resistance,

a. how far will the ball fall in one second?

b. how far will the ball fall in two seconds?

c. how far will the ball fall in five seconds?

d. when the ball has fallen 238.9632 meters, how long has it fallen?

64. The Central State Telephone Co. sent Mr. Abbott a bill. It showed the following: base charge, \$9.14; extra calls within Central State, \$3.48; calls to other states, \$12.79. There is a 4% Central State tax on all Central State calls, including the base charge. There is a 6% federal tax on all telephone charges except taxes. What was the total bill?

65. In 1975, California's population was estimated at 22,077,000. This was an increase of about $40\frac{1}{2}$ % over California's 1960 population. About how much was California's 1960 population?

66. Mr. Miller bought a $1\frac{1}{2}$-kilogram can of coffee for $8.70. On the average, he uses 4 grams of coffee to make a cup of coffee. What is his average cost of a cup of coffee?

67. The total length of a golf course is figured by taking the distance from each tee to each hole and adding all the distances. Hairy Mountain Golf Course, an 18-hole course, is 6524 yards long. What is the average length of each hole? (Your answer should include yards, feet, and inches.)

68. Mr. Kriss teaches history. He always grades test papers on "the curve." That is, the highest 10% of the paper's get A's, and the lowest 10% get E's. The next 15% on each end get B's or D's. The rest get C's. All of the twenty students in one of Mr. Kriss's classes took the test he gave two days ago. How many got A's? B's? C's? D's? E's?

69. You go shopping. You see two sizes of the same product. You can use either size without waste. Tell which size is the better buy.

	first size		**second size**	
	size	**price**	**size**	**price**
a.	280 g	2 for 57¢	420 g	3 for 1.15
b.	680 g	75¢	900 g	98¢
c.	700 g	48¢	1200 g	85¢
d.	284 g	2 for 49¢	400 g	3 for 99¢

70. You want to buy a motorcycle for \$800. The down payment is 30%. How much do you need for the down payment?

71. You drive from Big City to Smallville. You go the same speed all the way. It takes you $2\frac{1}{2}$ hours to get to the $\frac{1}{4}$ point. How long does it take you to get from Big City to the $\frac{3}{4}$ point?

72. Some years ago, the total value of goods produced in British Columbia was $2,906,962,000. Of this, 16% was forestry products, 14% was mineral products, 61% was manufactured products, 7% was agricultural products, and 2% was fish and fur products. What was the dollar value of the

a. forestry products?

b. mineral products?

c. manufactured products?

d. agricultural products?

e. fish and fur products?

73. Tomatoes sell at 2 cans for 55¢. How much will you be charged for 6 cans of tomatoes?

74. Twelve people can do a job in 4 days. How many people will it take (working at the same speed) to do the job in 3 days?

75. You buy some stock for $500. How much should you be able to sell it for now if the price is

a. 400% more?

b. 40% more?

c. .4% more?

76. A suit usually sells for $98.00. It is reduced in price by $\frac{1}{4}$.

a. How much is the discount?

b. What is the reduced price of the suit?

77. A store owner pays $225 for merchandise. To make a profit, he must sell it for at least 30% more than he pays. What is the least amount he must sell it for to show a profit?

78. It takes Mr. Jones 20% longer to do a job than it takes you to do it. You do the job in 30 minutes. How long does it take Mr. Jones to do the job?

79. At a supermarket, beets sell at 4 cans for 97¢. If you buy only one can of beets, how much will you be charged?

80. A student did 10 arithmetic problems. This was $\frac{2}{5}$ of the number assigned. How many problems were assigned?

81. You worked from 8:15 A.M. to 1:10 P.M. and from 1:35 P.M. to 5:25 P.M. How long did you work?

82. Ms. Kanten bought a set of tools for $750. She paid 25% down. There was a 16% yearly finance charge on the balance, which she agreed to pay in equal installments over a period of 18 months. How much was each monthly payment?

83. Imported ham sells for $1.19 a quarter-pound. How much will two pounds of it cost?

84. A bottle of shampoo costs $1.79 and lasts for 50 shampoos. A bottle of hair conditioner costs $2.78 and lasts for 75 treatments. Each time she shampoos her hair, Debby also uses the hair conditioner. Not counting the water used, what is the total cost of each of Debby's shampoos (to the nearest cent)?

85. Carpeting is on sale for $\frac{1}{3}$ off. A living room set is on sale for 20% off. Mr. and Mrs. Granler buy both. The usual price of the carpeting is $1,140. The usual price of the living room set is $900. How much do Mr. and Mrs. Granler pay?

86. Jerry wants to make a scale drawing of a side view of a car. The car is $5\frac{1}{2}$ meters long and $1\frac{1}{2}$ meters high. The paper Jerry has is 61 cm long and 30 cm wide. He wants to leave a margin of at least 3 cm all around the paper. What is the largest scale he can use?

87. At a supermarket, there is a 3% sales tax on everything sold except food. You go to this supermarket and buy items totaling $58.37 (not including sales tax). Of this amount, $29.58 is for food. The rest is not for food. How much is your total bill?

88. A wholesaler gives a store owner a 15% discount on the amount of a purchase. Besides this, a 20% discount is then given on the discounted price. The store owner's total purchase (before any discount) is $547.80. How much is he to pay the wholesaler?

89. Big City is 480 km from Ms. Jasper's home. On the way there, she drove at a steady speed of 80 kph. On the way back, she drove at a steady speed of 60 kph. What was her average speed for the round trip?

90. A ranch owner in Texas had 5,000 steers. He gave $\frac{1}{2}$ of them to his oldest son. He gave 30% of the rest to his brother. He sold $\frac{3}{14}$ of the number still left to another rancher. How many steers did he

a. give to his oldest son?

b. give to his brother?

c. sell to the other rancher?

d. end up with?

3. Mixed Concepts 3

INSTRUCTIONS

A. No problem is meant to trick you.

Example

Problem: You buy meat for $3.87. You give the cashier $5. How much change do you get?

Answer: $1.13 (Assume you pay the full price for the meat. Assume you don't buy anything else. Assume there is no sales tax. Assume the cashier gives you the correct change.)

B. You are given all the information you need to solve each problem.

Example

Problem: Oranges sell for 90¢ a dozen. You buy 8 oranges. You give the cashier 75¢. How much change do you get?

Answer: 15¢ (Assume you can buy part of a dozen at the price of 90¢ a dozen. Assume you don't buy anything else. Assume the cashier charges you the right amount. Assume the cashier gives you the right amount of change.)

C. If the answer is a fraction, write it in reduced form.

Example

Problem: Forty people shared 10 pies. How much did each person get?

Answer: $\frac{1}{4}$ pie (We get an answer of $\frac{10}{40}$ pie, which we reduce to $\frac{1}{4}$ pie.)

D. Do not round off any answer unless the problem makes it right to do so.

Example

Problem: Peas sell at 3 cans for $1.01. You buy one can of peas. How much will you be charged?

Answer: $.34 or 34¢ (You can't pay a store a fractional part of one cent.)

E. Assume that a business will always round a part of a cent up, not down, when you are to pay.

Example

Problem: Peas sell at 3 cans for $1. You buy one can of peas. How much will you be charged?

Answer: $.34 or 34¢ (not $.33 or 33¢—Also, you can't pay a store a fractional part of one cent.)

F. If an answer is not about money, and if the problem does not tell you how many decimal places to use, then carry the division to two decimal places unless you have a zero remainder before then.

Example

Problem: Write $\frac{49}{16}$ as a decimal.

Answer: $3.06\frac{1}{4}$ (not $3\frac{1}{16}$, not $3.0\frac{5}{8}$, not $3.062\frac{1}{2}$, and not 3.0625)

G. In general, if a percent is not a whole number, write the remainder as a fraction, not as a decimal.

Example

Problem: Rawlins earned $20,000 last year. This year she will earn $24,000. What percent of this year's earnings were last year's earnings?

Answer: $83\frac{1}{3}$% (not 83.3% or 83.33% or 83.333%, etc.)

1. One third of Mr. Harper's class are boys. 60% of Mr. Green's class are boys. There are 27 students in Mr. Harper's class. There are 25 students in Mr. Green's class. There are 6 boys who are in both Mr. Harper's and Mr. Green's classes. How many boys are in only one of the two classes?

2. A jetliner takes 4 hours and 15 minutes to fly from Detroit to Los Angeles. The air distance is 1,976 miles. What is the average speed of the plane (to the nearest tenth of a mile an hour)?

3. A pound of grass seed will seed 300 square feet of ground, if all the seeds germinate. Ms. Markey wants to seed her front and back yards. The front yard will be 50 feet by 30 feet. The back yard will be 40 feet by 60 feet. The seed she wants has a 90% germination rate. How many pounds should she buy? (Assume that she cannot buy a part of a pound.)

4. When driving his car, Mr. Tyler's reaction time between seeing a danger and hitting the brake pedal is $\frac{1}{2}$ second. If he drives 72 kph, how many meters does his car go in that $\frac{1}{2}$ second?

5. As shown below, a parking lot charges for time a car is parked there. The full amount is charged for any time in that price range. For example, if the charge is $1.00 an hour and you were parked there only $\frac{1}{2}$ hour, you still have to pay $1.00.

$1.50 for the first half-hour
$2.00 for the next hour
$1.00 for each of the next 3 hours
$ .50 for each of the next 19 hours
$ .50 for the next half-hour

The schedule starts over at the end of each 24-hour period. Tell how much the charge will be if you park your car in the lot for the times shown in each problem.

a. You park from 8:00 A.M. until 11:45 A.M.

b. You park from 9:15 A.M. until 4:48 P.M.

c. You park from 9:15 A.M. one day until 11:45 A.M. the next day.

d. You park from 8:37 A.M. until 2:15 P.M.

e. You park from 8:30 A.M. until 2:30 A.M.

6. Mr. Ino's class took a test. Half of the students scored at least 80%. Two-thirds of the others scored at least 70%. There were 30 students in the class. How many scored below 70%?

7. To figure out the selling price of groceries, a supermarket adds an average of 15% to its cost of the groceries. The market's sales of groceries one day totaled $5,060. How much was its profit on the groceries that day?

8. A racehorse averages 35 miles an hour when running around a one-mile track. How long (in minutes and/or seconds) does it take the horse to run the mile?

9. The circumference of a circular island is 7854 kilometers. Its area is 4,908.750 square kilometers. How long is its radius?

10. A car travels 600 kilometers at an average speed of 60 kph. On the return trip, the car averages 50 kph. What was its average speed for the entire 1200 kilometers?

11. A grocery owner buys a crate of apples for $9.72. The apples weigh 30 kilograms. The owner figures that 10% of the apples will spoil before they can be sold. The selling price of the apples which are to be sold must total $33\frac{1}{3}$ % more than the cost of the crate of apples. For how much a kilogram are the apples to be sold?

12. Juliet wants to make a muumuu. She can buy material either in a 1-meter width or in a $1\frac{1}{2}$-meter width. She figures she will need $4\frac{1}{2}$ meters of the 1-meter material, or she will need 3 meters of the $1\frac{1}{2}$-meter material. The 1-meter material sells for \$4.50 a meter. The $1\frac{1}{2}$-meter material sells for \$6.50 a meter.

a. Which material will cost Juliet less?

b. How much will she save if she buys this less expensive material?

13. A swimming pool is filled to an average depth of 8 feet. The pool is 30 feet wide and 50 feet long. There are 231 cubic inches of water in a gallon of water. How many gallons (to the nearest whole gallon) of water does it take to fill the pool?

14. The odometer and the speedometer of a car are both set in the factory. The factory sets them according to the size of the rear-wheel tire the car is supposed to use.

a. Your tire treads are worn down. The speedometer shows the car is going 60 kph. Is the car really going faster than, or slower than, 60 kph?

b. Your tire treads are worn down. The odometer shows the car traveled 10 kilometers. Did the car really travel more than, or less than, 10 kilometers?

c. You put larger (bigger diameter) tires on the rear wheels than the car manual says to use. Will the speedometer show a speed more than, or less than, the speed the car is really going? Explain.

15. The Cardenas Dam in Mexico is 787 feet long and 302 feet high. The volume of material in the dam is about 7,000,000 cubic yards. Suppose that the dam's vertical wall is the same width from bottom to top. Then how many feet wide is the dam (to the nearest whole foot)?

16. Ms. Andrews stays in a hotel room for 3 days. There is a 9% state tax on room rentals. The room charge is $35 a day, not including the tax. She also charges $8.45 in telephone calls and $25.67 in meals to her room. How much is her total hotel bill?

17. Mr. Zender stays in a hotel room for 4 days. There is a 9% state tax on room rentals. His total bill is $192.24, including the room, the tax, and each of the following: $9.34 a day for meals; $2.75 a day for phone calls.

a. How much is the charge for his room, including the tax?

b. How much is the tax?

18. The local ice cream store gives you a choice of ice cream cones. You can get a cone with two scoops of ice cream for 50¢, or you can get a cone with three scoops of ice cream for 60¢. The diameter of a scoop for the two-scoop cone is $2\frac{3}{4}$ inches. The diameter of a scoop for the three-scoop cone is $2\frac{1}{2}$ inches. Which cone gives you more ice cream for your money? (The formula for the volume of a sphere is $V = \frac{4}{3}\pi r^3$.)

19. A lever balances on a fulcrum. When you push down on one end, the other end goes up. The part of the lever between you and the fulcrum is called the effort arm. The part between the fulcrum and the other end is called the load arm. The length of the effort arm times the amount of effort on it equals the length of the load arm times the amount of effort on it. (Example: Suppose the effort arm is 3 feet long and the load arm is 2 feet long. If you put 10 pounds of weight on the effort arm, it will lift 15 pounds of weight. This is, 3 feet × 10 pounds = 2 feet × 15 pounds.)

a. The effort arm of a 5-foot lever is 3 feet long. You apply 50 pounds to the effort arm. How many pounds will the load arm lift?

b. The effort arm of a 5-foot lever is 4 feet long. You apply 50 pounds to the effort arm. How many pounds will the load arm lift?

c. You have a 4-foot crowbar and want to move a 300-pound rock. You are able to use 100 pounds of effort. Where should you place the fulcrum?

d. Zora and Jeff want to play on a seesaw. The seesaw is 10 feet long. Zora weighs 75 pounds. Jeff weighs 50 pounds. How far from Zora should the fulcrum be?

20. The lengths of the shadows cast by two objects in the sun is directly proportional to the heights of the objects. That is, $\frac{\text{length of shadow of \#1}}{\text{length of shadow of \#2}} = \frac{\text{height of \#1}}{\text{height of \#2}}$.

a. Royce is $5\frac{1}{2}$ feet tall. His shadow is 4 feet long. The shadow of the tree in his front yard is 20 feet long. How high is the top of the tree?

b. Jane is 155 cm tall. A 620-cm flagpole's shadow is 500 cm long. How long is Jane's shadow?

21. In astronomy, a light year is the distance light travels in a year. The speed of light is 299,792 kilometers a second.

a. How far is a light year? (Use $365\frac{1}{4}$ days for year.)

b. Earth is an average distance of 149,590,000 kilometers from the sun. How long (in minutes and seconds) does it take light to reach Earth from the sun?

22. In a bowling league, the largest ball permitted has a circumference of 60 cm. To the nearest tenth, what is the volume of this ball? (Use $\pi = 3.1416$.)

23. Ms. Sanders ate at a restaurant. She spent a total of $9.00, including a tip of 20% on the cost of the meal.

a. How much was the meal?

b. How much was the tip?

24. In a bowling league, a "spot" between two teams is figured as follows: For each team, the league averages of its members are totaled. The spot is 70% (to the nearest whole number) of the difference. Team A will bowl against Team B tomorrow. The league averages of Team A's members are 170, 169, 194, 175, and 167. The league averages of Team B's members are 165, 160, 191, 187, and 154. How much is the spot?

25. In business, "gross profit" and "markup" are the same in dollars, but they are different in percents. In dollars, they are the difference between selling price and cost of goods. This difference is then used to figure the two percents needed. It is done as follows: (1) The percent of gross profit is the difference between selling price and cost of goods times 100% divided by the selling price. (2) The percent of markup is the same difference times 100% divided by the cost.

Example: A grocery store pays $100 for food and sells it for $125. Both the gross profit and the markup are $25. The percent of gross profit is $\frac{\$25 \times 100\%}{\$125} = 20\%$ and the percent of markup is $\frac{\$25 \times 100\%}{\$100} = 25\%$.

Based on $100 for the cost of goods, figure out the missing percents below.

% of gross profit	% of markup
a. 10	
b. 15	
c. 20	
d. 25	
e. 30	
f. $33\frac{1}{3}$	
g. 40	
h. 50	
i. $66\frac{2}{3}$	
j. 75	

26. Use the figures from problem 25.

a. A businessperson pays $100 for goods. A gross profit of $33\frac{1}{3}$ % is needed. How much should the selling price be?

b. A grocery owner pays $3.65 for a 24-can case of spinach. A gross profit of 20% is needed. What should be the selling price for a can of spinach?

c. A novelty store pays $35.50 for 100 novelty items. All are to be sold at the same price. A 75% gross profit is needed. What should be the selling price of each item?

27. The amount of light reaching a place varies in inverse proportion to the square of the distance from the light source. (That is, the light is brighter when you are close to it, and it is dimmer when you are far from it.) Ann is 60 cm away from a light source. Ken is 90 cm away from the same light source. How many times brighter is it where Ann is than where Ken is?

28. Mr. Sherber is going to plant flower seeds along a 35-meter lawn border. Each package of seeds will cover about $1\frac{1}{2}$ meters of the border if all the seeds germinate. How many packages of seeds should he buy if the seeds have an 85% germination rate?

29. A telephone company has three kinds of dial-direct rates: weekday (full rate); evening (35% discount from the full rate); night and weekend (60% discount from the full rate). The weekday rate is used Monday through Friday, 8:00 A.M. to 5:00 P.M. The evening rate is used Sunday through Friday, 5:00 P.M. to 11:00 P.M. The night and weekend rate is used all other times. The charge is based on the time the call is answered, not the time the call is ended. (For example, a Monday call answered at 4:55 P.M. and ended at 5:15 P.M. is charged at the weekday rate.) The following weekday rates are in effect for calls from Big City:

To	First Minute	Each Additional Minute
Atlanta	50¢	34¢
Chicago	46¢	32¢
Denver	52¢	36¢
Seattle	54¢	38¢

Any part of a minute is charged as a full minute. Find the charge on each of the following calls from Big City.

a. On Sunday Mr. Wilson dials a number in Seattle at 9:00 A.M. The call is answered immediately. The call is over at 9:17 A.M. How much is the charge?

b. Mr. Wilson calls the same number at 6:00 P.M. the same day. The connection lasts for 17 minutes. How much is the charge?

c. The next day, Mr. Wilson calls the same number again. This time the call is made at 10:00 A.M. Again, the call lasts for 17 minutes. How much is the charge?

d. On Wednesday, Ms. Young's dialed call to Chicago is answered at 9:00 A.M. The call is finished at 9:25 A.M. How much is the charge?

e. On Friday, Ms. Joplin's dialed call to Denver is answered at 5:07 P.M. Both parties hang up at 5:58 P.M. How much is the charge?

f. On Monday, Mr. Horner dials Atlanta at 11:10 P.M., and his party answers right away. They hang up at 11:33 P.M. How much is the charge?

30. Everyday Finance Co. loans money. Monthly interest on the unpaid balance is charged as follows: $2\frac{1}{2}$ % on the first \$100; 2% on the next \$150; $1\frac{1}{2}$ % on the next \$150; $1\frac{1}{4}$ % on any balance over \$400. Mr. and Mrs. Marner borrow \$500 from Everyday Finance Co. Their monthly payments are \$90, including interest. Complete the schedule below.

Date of Payment	Total Payment	Interest	Principal	Balance Due
3/15	Amount Borrowed			\$500.00
4/15	\$90.00			
5/15	\$90.00			
6/15	\$90.00			
7/15	\$90.00			
8/15	\$90.00			

31. Mr. and Mrs. Kramer also borrow $500 from Everyday Finance Co. Their monthly payments are also $90, including interest. A "month" has the number of days there are from one payment date to the same day the next month. (In the problem on the previous page, the "month" from the 4/15 to the 5/15 payment has 30 days. The "month" from the 5/15 payment to the 6/15 payment has 31 days.) If a payment is made early or late, then the interest charge is adjusted accordingly. For example, if the 6/15 payment is made on 6/20, then interest is charged for an extra 5 days. That is, the interest charge is $\frac{36}{31}$ of the normal interest charge. Fill in the schedule below.

Date of Payment	Total Payment	Interest	Principal	Balance Due
3/15	Amount Borrowed			$500.00
4/10	$90.00			
5/20	$90.00			
6/25	$90.00			
7/15	$90.00			
8/25	$90.00			

32. A covered truck bed is 7 feet wide, 12 feet long, and 6 feet high. It is to be loaded with packing crates which are $1\frac{1}{2}$ feet wide, 3 feet long, and $1\frac{3}{4}$ feet high.

a. What is the capacity (volume) of the truck bed?

b. What is the volume of each packing crate?

c. How many whole packing crates can be fitted in the truck bed?

d. What volume of the truck bed will be unused after the packing crates are fitted in?

33. Mr. Eaton drove his car on a 600-kilometer trip. He drove 80 kilometers an hour for $\frac{2}{3}$ of the way, and he drove 60 kilometers an hour the rest of the way.

a. How long did the trip take him?

b. What was his average speed?

34. A covered truck bed is 7 feet wide, 12 feet long, and 6 feet high. It is to be loaded with packing crates which are $1\frac{3}{4}$ feet wide, 3 feet long, and $1\frac{3}{4}$ feet high.

a. What is the capacity (volume) of the truck bed?

b. What is the volume of each packing crate?

c. How many whole packing crates can be fitted in the truck bed?

d. What volume of the truck bed will be unused after the packing crates are fitted in?

35. A jetliner left the St. Louis air terminal at 7:00 P.M. and arrived at a Detroit air terminal at 9:05 P.M. The distance between the air terminals is 462 miles.

a. To the nearest tenth, what was the average speed of the jetliner?

b. To the nearest whole number, what was the average speed of the jetliner?

36. A salesperson was to attend a convention in a distant city. Her boss asked how much it would probably cost. The salesperson figured the following: air fare, \$250; hotel bill, 4 days at \$35, plus 8% room tax; meals, 13 at \$4.50; mileage to and from the airport, 70 miles at 20¢ a mile; airport parking fee, \$9.75; telephone calls, \$15; miscellaneous, \$10. Suppose these figures were correct. How much did it cost the company to have the salesperson attend the convention (not counting the salesperson's salary or the sales lost because the salesperson was at the convention)?

37. A supermarket makes a gross profit of 5% on coffee and on soap. It makes a 20% gross profit on canned vegetables and soup. It makes a 30% gross profit on fresh fruits and vegetables. The market's sales one day were as follows: canned vegetables, $300; coffee, $200; fresh vegetables, $100; canned soup, $150; soap, $350; fresh fruit, $150. How much was the market's total gross profit on these items that day?

38. You want to tile a room which is 20 feet by 30 feet. The tiles are each 9 inches square. You may have to cut some tiles. But you do not want to put two or more part-tiles together to make either a whole tile or another part-tile.

a. What is the area of the room to be tiled?

b. How many tiles will it take to do the job the way you want to do it?

c. The tiles are on sale for $1.75 a dozen. How many dozen will you need to buy?

d. How much will the tile cost?

39. A room is 14 feet 5 inches by 15 feet 7 inches. What is its area (in square feet)?

40. You are payroll clerk in a company. Workers are paid three rates: straight time (the hourly rate); time and a half ($1\frac{1}{2}$ times the hourly rate); double time (twice the hourly rate).

A worker gets straight time except as follows. The worker gets time and a half for any time worked over 8 hours in one day or for any work on a Saturday. The worker gets double time for any time worked on a Sunday or a holiday or for any time worked over 8 hours on a Saturday. (If a holiday falls on, say, Tuesday, then the worker gets double time for all time worked that Tuesday.)

In each problem which follows, you are given the worker's hourly rate and the number of hours worked each day in the week. An asterisk (*) following a number of hours means that that day was a holiday. Figure out each worker's gross pay (that is, the pay before any payroll deductions for taxes, etc.). Show all of your work.

	Hourly Rate	Sun.	Mon.	Tues.	Wed.	Thurs.	Fri.	Sat.	Gross Pay
a.	$4.50	0	8	8	8	8	8	0	
b.	$4.50	0	10	8	8	8	8	0	
c.	$4.50	0	0	8	8	8	8	8	
d.	$4.50	8	8	8	8	8	8	8	
e.	$4.50	8	10	12	8	6	10	10	
f.	$4.50	8	8*	10	10	8	10	8	
g.	$5.82	8	8	10	8	8	8	10	
h.	$6.75	0	0	0	10	12*	10	10	
i.	$7.85	2	8	8	7	9	10	6	

41. You are still a payroll clerk for the same company. The company installs a time clock for its hourly workers. Overtime rates are the same as before. Time is computed to $\frac{1}{10}$ of an hour. When punching in, a worker is allowed a two-minute leeway for each $\frac{1}{10}$-hour period. After that two minutes, the worker is counted as arriving in the next $\frac{1}{10}$-hour period. (If Mr. Smith punches in at 8:02 A.M., he is paid starting at 8:00 A.M. If he punches in from 8:03 A.M. to 8:08 A.M., he is paid starting at 8:06 A.M.) When punching out, the worker is paid to the last previous $\frac{1}{10}$-hour period unless the time falls on a $\frac{1}{10}$-hour period. (If Ms. Jones punches out at any time from 4:00 P.M. to 4:05 P.M., she is paid until 4:00 P.M. If she punches out at any time from 4:06 P.M. until 4:11 P.M., she is paid until 4:06 P.M.)

In the chart which follows, read down for each problem. You are given the hourly rate, the time punched in, and the time punched out for each day. Figure out each worker's gross pay for the week. Show all of your work.

Problem	a.	b.	c.	d.	e.
Hourly Rate	$5.76	$8.19	$7.75	$4.50	$5.10
Sun.		I 7:00 O 2:00	I 6:30 O 11:30 I 12:18 O 4:00	I 6:30 O 11:30 I 12:12 O 4:00	I 6:30 O 11:30 I 12:30 O 4:02
Mon.	I 8:24 O 12:00 I 12:30 O 4:30	I 8:00 O 12:00 I 1:00 O 5:00	I 6:30 O 11:30 I 12:18 O 4:00	I 6:30 O 11:30 I 12:12 O 4:00	I 6:32 O 11:36 I 12:30 O 4:06
Tues.	I 10:12 O 2:00	I 9:00 O 1:00		I 7:45 O 11:30 I 1:00 O 5:05	
Wed.			I 7:35 O 11:35		
Thurs.	I 6:30 O 10:30				I 6:40 O 10:40
Fri.			I 6:30 O 10:30		
Sat.	I 6:30 O 11:30	I 7:00 O 11:05	I 8:03 O 11:30		

42. A nationwide trucking company picks up and delivers packages anywhere in the continental United States except Alaska. The fee for this service depends on the weight of the package and the distance it is to be delivered.

- First, there is a service charge of $2.00.
- Next, there is a weight charge as follows:

  $2.00 for the first kilogram

  $1.00/kilogram for each of the next 5 kilograms

  $ .50/kilogram for each kilogram over 6 kilograms

  The weight charge is not adjusted for fractional kilograms. For example, the weight charge for a 3-kilogram package would be the same as for a $2\frac{1}{2}$-kilogram package—that is, $4.00.

- The base charge is the total of the service charge and the weight charge.
- Finally, the distance charge is as follows:

Distance in km		**Add this percent of base charge**
at least	**but less than**	
0	15	0
15	80	20
80	160	30
160	400	40
400	800	50
800	1600	65
1600	2400	80
2400	3200	95
over 3200		110

Example Problem:

A 5-kilogram package is to be delivered a distance of 95 kilometers. What is the trucking company's charge?

Solution:

$2.00 service charge
$6.00 weight charge ($2.00 + 4 × $1.00)
$8.00 base charge
$2.40 distance charge (add 30% of base charge)
$10.40 total charge

For each problem below, compute the trucking company's charge. Show your work.

a. A 5-kg package is to be delivered a distance of 500 km.

b. A 9-kg package is to be delivered a distance of 10 km.

c. A 7-kg package is to be delivered a distance of 1600 km.

d. A $6\frac{1}{2}$-kg package is to be delivered a distance of 25 km.

e. A 12.4-kg package is to be delivered a distance of 2400 km.

f. A 3.4-kg package is to be delivered a distance of 98 km.

43. These problems will give you practice in figuring out a bowling score. For each problem, use a bowling score sheet like the ones shown, and show the running score.

SCORING

Bowling is scored in "frames." There are 10 frames per game, and each bowler receives two tries per frame to knock down as many of the 10 pins as possible. There are three scoring possibilities per frame: (1) the bowler knocks down fewer than 10 pins with two balls, (2) the bowler knocks down all 10 pins with two balls (a spare), (3) the bowler knocks down all 10 pins with the first ball (a strike).

A strike counts as 10 pins plus the total number of pins that the bowler knocks down with the next two balls. A spare counts as 10 pins plus the number of pins the bowler knocks down with the next ball.

If the bowler scores a strike or a spare in the tenth frame, he or she rolls extra balls. If the bowler scores a strike on the first ball in the 10th frame, he or she receives two extra throws. If the bowler scores a spare in the 10th frame, he or she receives one extra throw. A bowler never bowls more than three balls in the 10th frame.

USING THE SCORE SHEET

Frames are represented on the score sheet by ten numbered, divided boxes (see below). Each frame on the score sheet (except the tenth) has two small boxes for recording the numbers of pins knocked down in that frame and a larger open area for keeping track of the running score. There are three small squares in the last frame to accommodate the extra throws awarded to bowlers bowling a strike or a spare in the 10th frame.

The pins knocked down are indicated in the two small squares at the top right corner of each frame. The three possible scores are shown on the score sheet as follows: (1) When fewer than 10 pins are knocked down, the number of pins knocked down with the first ball is written in the first (leftmost) small square, and the number of pins knocked down with the second ball is written in the second small square. If no pins are knocked down with a particular ball, a dash is entered in the small square. (2) When a spare is thrown, the number of pins knocked down with the first ball goes in the first small square, as usual, and a diagonal line is used in the second small square. (3) A strike is shown by marking an X in the first of the two small squares. The second small square remains blank.

The running total for the score is written in the larger space of each frame. After frame 1, the total for each new frame is added to the totals of the previous frames to get a running total. Note that you can't add the total for strikes or spares into the running total until all the balls that count for the strike's or spare's score have been played. In an actual game, the figure for the running total may be one or two frames behind the frame of play.

1	2	3	4	5	6	7	8	9	10	Total

a. The table below shows the results of a game of bowling. Fill in the score sheet, and find the total score.

Frame	First Ball	Second Ball
1	5	4
2	7	3
3	10	
4	8	2
5	10	
6	10	
7	10	
8	7	3
9	6	3
10	4	3

1	2	3	4	5	6	7	8	9	10	Total

b. The table below shows the results of a game of bowling. Fill in the score sheet, and find the total score.

Frame	First Ball	Second Ball	
1	10		
2	10		
3	7	2	
4	6	3	
5	9	1	
6	9	1	
7	8	2	
8	10		
9	10		
10	8	2	Third ball = 9

1	2	3	4	5	6	7	8	9	10	Total

c. What is the maximum possible score a bowler can receive? Show on the score sheet how this score would be recorded.

1	2	3	4	5	6	7	8	9	10	Total

Answers

1: Mixed Concepts 1

1. 35
2. 3
3. 625
4. 24
5. $1\frac{1}{2}$
6. 22
7. 1174
8. 11
9. 90 miles
10. 25¢
11. 40
12. 2078 miles
13. 60
14. 30
15. 34
16. 1020 grams
17. 102
18. $1.20
19. 15
20. 360 feet
21. 375
22. 11
23. 36
24. 450
25. 63,360
26. 300
27. 71¢
28. $90.50
29. 14
30. $145.25
31. 85%
32. $3.10
33. $952
34. $7.50
35. 18
36. $11.97
37. **a.** $2.00 **b.** $33\frac{1}{3}$¢ **c.** 34¢
38. $1.55
39. 65
40. 520
41. $1\frac{1}{2}$ cups
42. $12\frac{1}{2}$
43. $195
44. $6.80
45. 600 km an hour
46. 4 seconds
47. 188
48. 4 hours 15 minutes
49. 4
50. 40
51. 60
52. 6.6
53. 240,000
54. $3.90
55. 8
56. $168
57. 671 miles
58. $8\frac{1}{2}$
59. $62.40
60. 80 kilometers an hour
61. $1,500,000
62. 225 kilometers
63. 2555 or 2562, depending on whether or not the year was leap year
64. $88.36
65. $3.33
66. 8
67. $280
68. $9.18
69. 8708 feet
70. 380
71. $14\frac{7}{12}$¢
72. 10 cm
73. $11.11
74. **a.** $1.27 **b.**$1.28
75. 880 sq. ft.
76. 21.5
77. **a.** 10 cm **b.** 40 cm
78. **a.** 6 kg **b.** 9 kg
79. 40%
80. more than $2,916,666\frac{2}{3}$ bushels
81. $133\frac{1}{3}$
82. 38.1
83. **a.** $1.15 **b.** $57\frac{1}{2}$¢
84. 8,136,396 sq. km
85. 145
86. $62\frac{1}{2}$
87. $8.40
88. 100
89. 61.2
90. 3,800,000
91. about 3,223,950
92. $7.30
93. 12
94. $724,832.21
95. 828
96. about $4,656,862.75
97. $53\frac{11}{13}$%
98. $559\frac{6}{13}$ sq. km
99. 171,429
100. $37\frac{1}{2}$
101. 28 cm by 38 cm
102. by 114,378
103. 25.1328 meters
104. 90
105. The first area is a square with each side 4 kilometers long, so it has an area of 16 square kilometers. The second area can be any shape and is 4

square kilometers in area. The first area is 12 square kilometers larger than the second.

106. 176,735.59 sq. km

107. **a.** $24,161,000,000 **b.** $6\frac{489}{6431}$ %

108. **a.** about 24% **b.** about 5,520,000

109. 35,714

110. 110,942 sq. km

111. $55\frac{5}{9}$ %

112. 6156 cu. cm

113. 531

114. by about 1,540,000

115. $9\frac{13}{18}$ ¢

116. 7 strokes over par

117. 70 kph

118. 320 km

119. $2.00

120. 307

121. **a.** 439 **b.** 1317

122. 2420

123. $7.80

124. $1,250

125. $217.50

126. $63

127. 7.2

128. 4 teaspoons of sugar

129. $12.16

130. 54

131. $8\frac{2}{3}$ %

132. 28%

133. 54¢

134. $11,200

135. about 15,789

136. $17\frac{1}{2}$ ft.

2: Mixed Concepts 2

1. 5 km

2. $5.38

3. $586.26

4. $1,920

5. 448 sq. ft.

6. gross pay = $224.80; federal income tax = $40.46; state income tax = $11.24; social security tax = $13.71; union dues = $2.25; net pay = $157.14

7. **a.** $6\frac{2}{5}$ **b.** $7.36

8. 50 words a minute

9. $37.50

10. 720,000

11. 800 sq. cm

12. 80

13. She pays $44.24 less if she pays cash.

14. $2\frac{1}{2}$ yards

15. The first brand is the better buy.

16. $20\frac{1}{2}$ hours

17. $1,170 (Note: This is a good opportunity to stress to your students that there are $4\frac{1}{3}$, not 4, weeks in a month.)

18. 4

19. 28

20. $21\frac{2}{3}$ ¢

21. **a.** neither **b.** The gold is heavier. (Note: An apothecaries' ounce is actually slightly heavier than an avoirdupois ounce.)

22. **a.** $6650 **b.** $4500

23. 6 hr. 33 min.

24. 5 hr. 27 min.

25. Jay; 1 hr. 6 min.

26. $197.75

27. $181.00

28. **a.** 80,776,500 **b.** 66,775,240 **c.** 40,926,760

29. **a.** 532 **b.** 266

30. .310

31. 11

32. 4,320

33. $2.27

34. **a.** $3679.97 **b.** $3692.98 **c.** salesman 2

35. 220,000 sq. cm

36. **a.** $\frac{14}{24}$ or $\frac{7}{12}$ **b.** $41\frac{2}{3}$ %

37. $634.00

38. Mr. Whitney paid 40¢ more.

39. **a.** 14.20 **b.** 11.07 **c.** 97.5 **d.** 78.0 **e.** 886 ft. **f.** 1420 ft.

40. $937.73

41. 3 inches by $3\frac{3}{4}$ inches

42. **a.** 77.4% **b.** 77.4%

43. $1061.37

44. $19.00

45. She ends up getting the same amount for the money spent with both brands.

46. $35 billion

47. 89.4%

48. 9.0

49. 15 years 11 months

50. **a.** 19¢ **b.** $1.26 or $1.27, depending on whether the telephone company rounds to the nearest cent or charges the next higher cent for any amount which is not an exact number of cents

51. $350

52. 17.6 feet

53. 47% aluminum; 3.5% silica; 2% titanium

oxide; 22% iron oxide; 25.5% water

54. **a.** $70 **b.** $334 **c.** $1,036

55. $215.35

56. **a.** $46\frac{3}{4}$ **b.** $42\frac{1}{2}$

57. $\frac{4}{5}$

58. **a.** 6579% **b.** $149\frac{23}{44}$ %

59. $1,050

60. $846.75

61. **a.** 22 **b.** 400,000 **c.** 1,600,000 **d.** $72{,}727\frac{3}{11}$ **e.** $18{,}181\frac{9}{11}$ **f.** 4

62. $33,823,529,411.76

63. **a.** 4.8768 meters **b.** 19.5072 meters **c.** 121.92 meters **d.** 7 seconds

64. $27.43

65. 15,713,167

66. 2.32¢

67. 362 yards 1 foot 4 inches

68. 2; 3; 10; 3; 2

69. **a.** second size **b.** second size **c.** first size **d.** second size

70. $240

71. $7\frac{1}{2}$ hours

72. **a.** $465,113,920 **b.** $406,974,680 **c.** $1,773,246,820 **d.** $203,487,340 **e.** $58,139,240

73. $1.65

74. 16

75. **a.** $2,500 **b.** $700 **c.** $502

76. **a.** $24.50 **b.** $73.50

77. $292.50

78. 36 minutes

79. 25¢ (Point out to your students that stores do not round prices to the nearest cent but charge the next higher cent on any price which is not an exact number of cents.)

80. 25

81. 8 hrs. 45 min. or $8\frac{3}{4}$ hrs.

82. $38.75

83. $9.52

84. 7¢

85. $1,480

86. 1 cm in the drawing = 10 cm on the car

87. $59.23

88. $372.50

89. $68\frac{4}{7}$ kph

90. **a.** 2500 **b.** 750 **c.** 375 **d.** 1375

3: Mixed Concepts 3

1. 12

2. 464.9 mph

3. 15

4. 10

5. **a.** $6.50 **b.** $8.50 **c.** $21 **d.** $7.50 **e.** $13.50

6. 5

7. $660

8. 1 min. $42\frac{6}{7}$ sec.

9. 1250 km

10. $54\frac{6}{11}$ kph

11. 48¢

12. **a.** The $1\frac{1}{2}$ meter material will cost less. **b.** 75¢

13. 89,766

14. **a.** slower **b.** less **c.** The speedometer will show a speed less than the real speed of the car. The speedometer is set to register according to the rate at which the rear wheels turn. For each turn, the wheels are traveling farther with the large tires than they would with the regulation tires. Thus, when the speedometer is showing, say, 60 kph, the car is going farther than 60 kilometers every hour and so is traveling faster than 60 kph

15. 795 ft.

16. $148.57

17. **a.** $143.88 **b.** $11.88

18. the 2-scoop cone

19. **a.** 75 lbs. **b.** 200 lbs. **c.** at most 1 foot from the rock **d.** 4 feet

20. **a.** $27\frac{1}{2}$ feet **b.** 125 cm

21. **a.** 9,460,716,019,200 km **b.** 8 min. $18\frac{18349}{18737}$ sec.

22. 3647.6 cu. cm

23. **a.** $7.50 **b.** $1.50

24. 13

25. **a.** $11\frac{1}{9}$ **b.** $17\frac{11}{17}$ **c.** 25 **d.** $33\frac{1}{3}$ **e.** $42\frac{6}{7}$ **f.** 50 **g.** $66\frac{2}{3}$ **h.** 100 **i.** 200 **j.** 300

26. **a.** $150 **b.** 19¢ **c.** $1.42

27. $2\frac{1}{4}$

28. 28

29. **a.** $2.65 **b.** $4.30

c. $6.62 **d.** $8.14
e. $12.04 **f.** $3.19

30. See table at right
31. See table at right
32. **a.** 504 cu. ft.
b. $7\frac{7}{8}$ cu. ft. **c.** 64, but they must be stacked on their sides rather than on their bottoms
d. none
33. **a.** 8 hr. 20 min.
b. 72 km an hour
34. **a.** 504 cu. ft.
b. $9\frac{3}{16}$ cu. ft.
c. 48, whether they are stacked on bottoms, sides, or ends.
d. 63 cu. ft.
35. **a.** 426.5 mph (Note: Since St. Louis is on Central time and Detroit is on Eastern time, the flight time was 1 hr. 5 min., not 2 hr. 5 min.)
b. 426 mph
36. $508.45
37. $192.50
38. **a.** 600 sq. ft. **b.** 1080
c. 90 **d.** $157.50
39. $224\frac{95}{144}$ sq. ft.

30. Answer table

Date of Payment	**Total Payment**	**Interest**	**Principal**	**Balance Due**
3/15	Amount Borrowed			$500.00
4/15	$90.00	$9.00	$81.00	$419.00
5/15	$90.00	7.99	82.01	336.99
6/15	$90.00	6.80	83.20	253.79
7/15	$90.00	5.56	84.44	169.35
8/15	$90.00	3.89	86.11	83.24

31. Answer table

Date of Payment	**Total Payment**	**Interest**	**Principal**	**Balance Due**	**Part of Month**
3/15	Amount Borrowed			$500.00	---
4/10	$90.00	$ 7.55	$82.45	$417.55	26/31
5/20	$90.00	10.63	79.37	338.18	40/30
6/25	$90.00	7.92	82.08	256.10	36/31
7/15	$90.00	3.73	86.27	169.83	20/30
8/25	$90.00	5.15	84.85	84.98	41/31

40. See table next page
41. The number of hours to be paid is shown in the table at right.
42. **a.** $12 **b.** $10.50
c. $17.10 **d.** $11.40
e. $24.38 **f.** $9.10.
43. **a.** Score = 178
See table next page
b. Score = 188
See table next page
c. Highest possible score = 300
See table next page

40. Answer table

	Hourly Rate	Sun.	Mon.	Tues.	Wed.	Thurs.	Fri.	Sat.	Straight Time	Time and a Half	Double Time	Gross Pay
a.	$4.50	0	8	8	8	8	8	0	40	0	0	$180.00
b.	$4.50	0	10	8	8	8	8	0	40	2	0	193.50
c.	$4.50	0	0	8	8	8	8	8	32	8	0	198.00
d.	$4.50	8	8	8	8	8	8	8	40	8	8	306.00
e.	$4.50	8	10	12	8	6	10	10	38	16	10	369.00
f.	$4.50	8	8*	10	10	8	10	8	32	14	16	382.50
g.	$5.82	8	8	10	8	8	8	10	40	10	10	436.50
h.	$6.75	0	0	0	10	12*	10	10	16	12	14	418.50
i.	$7.85	2	8	8	7	9	10	6	39 3/4	10	2 1/2	469.04

41. Answer table

Problem	a.	b.	c.	d.	e.
Hourly Rate	$5.76	$8.19	$7.75	$4.50	$5.10
Sun.	0	7	5 + 3.7	5 + 3.8	5 + 3.5
Mon.	3.6 + 4	4 + 4	5 + 3.7	5 + 3.8	5.1 + 3.6
Tues.	3.8	4	0	3.7 + 4	0
Wed.	0	0	3.9	0	0
Thurs.	4	0	0	0	4.9
Fri.	0	0	4	0	0
Sat.	5	4	2.9	0	0
Standard Time	15.4	12	15.9	15.7	12.9
Time and a Half	5	4	3.6	.8	.7
Double Time	0	7	8.7	8.8	8.5
Gross Pay	$131.90	$262.08	$299.93	$155.25	$157.85

43a. Answer table

1	2	3	4	5	6	7	8	9	10	Total
5 4	7	X	8	X	X	X	7	6 3	4 3 —	178
9	29	49	69	99	126	146	162	171	178	

43b. Answer table

1	2	3	4	5	6	7	8	9	10	Total
X	X	7 2	6 3	9	9	8	X	X	8 9	188
27	46	55	64	83	101	121	149	169	188	

43c. Answer table

1	2	3	4	5	6	7	8	9	10	Total
X	X	X	X	X	X	X	X	X	X X X	300
30	60	90	120	150	180	210	240	270	300	

